D1715529

Young Heroes

Matt Dalio

China Care Founder

Michael V. Uschan

KIDHAVEN PRESS
An imprint of Thomson Gale, a part of The Thomson Corporation

THOMSON

GALE™

Detroit • New York • San Francisco • New Haven, Conn. • Waterville, Maine • London

For more information, contact:
KidHaven Press
27500 Drake Rd.
Farmington Hills, MI 48331-3535
Or you can visit our Internet site at http://www.gale.com

LIBRARY OF CONGRESS CATALOGING-IN-PUBLICATION DATA

Uschan, Michael V., 1948–
    Matt Dalio : China Care founder / by Michael V. Uschan.
        p. cm. — (Young heroes)
    Includes bibliographical references and index.
    ISBN 978-0-7377-3670-0 (hardcover)
    1. Dalio, Matt, 1984– 2. China Care (Organization) 3. Young volunteers in social service—United States—Juvenile literature. 4. Orphans—Care—China. 5. Charities—China. I. Title.
    HV28.D27U73 2007
    362.73092—dc22
    [B]
                                                                2007007780

ISBN-10: 0-7377-3670-4

Printed in the United States of America

Contents

Helping Those Who Need Help the Most

In 2000 Matt Dalio visited the People's Republic of China during his summer vacation. The sixteen-year-old from Greenwich, Connecticut, had already traveled there many times. He had even lived in Beijing from 1995 to 1996.

Matt went back to China in 2000 to find out about the country's many **orphans**. He visited **orphanages** and talked to people who worked in them. Matt was saddened to learn that millions of boys and girls were growing up without families. He discovered that many orphans had physical and mental **disabilities** but were not getting the medical care they needed. He also saw that many of the orphanages were overcrowded and in poor repair.

The teenager decided to help Chinese orphans. When he returned home, Matt started China Care. The **charitable foundation** raises money,

As a teenager, Matt Dalio founded China Care after learning of the struggles facing many Chinese orphans.

collects supplies, and provides medical care for disabled orphans in China. It also helps U.S. citizens to **adopt** children from China and Chinese people to become **foster families** so that even orphans who aren't adopted can live with a family instead of at an orphanage.

Matt has a simple explanation for why he decided to do what he did: "The orphans in China had absolutely nothing—they were at the bottom of the heap, unable to fight for themselves and without anyone to fight for them. I just wanted to help them." [1]

Chapter One

Matt Dalio Learns to Love China

Matt Dalio was born on January 29, 1984. He went to the People's Republic of China for the first time on a family vacation in 1987, when he was only three years old. His parents could not know it at the time, but that visit was the first of many that would make their son grow to love the far-off country.

Matt's Family

Matt grew up in Greenwich, Connecticut. His parents are Raymond and Barbara Dalio and he has three brothers—Devon, Paul, and Mark. Matt is the third-oldest child in the Dalio family.

His father owns Bridgewater Associates, a company that helps people make **investments** in foreign countries. Raymond's successful business made enough money to give his family a comfortable lifestyle. The Dalios lived in a large home, and Matt and his brothers attended private schools where they received a fine education.

Raymond Dalio's work required him to travel to foreign countries. He sometimes took his family with him so that the business trips could also be family vacations. Raymond did this in 1987 when he went to China to give officials of that country advice on making investments. The Dalios stayed in China for a month. Raymond continued to do business in China after the 1987 trip, and over the next few years Matt and his family traveled there several more times.

Each time Matt visited China, he became more interested in the country and its people. In 1995 his desire to learn more about China led him to do something that

Matt Dalio attended the sixth grade while living in Beijing, China. One of China's most well-known attractions, the Great Wall of China, pictured, runs along Beijing.

most young people can only dream about—live in a foreign country.

Matt Moves to China

Matt lived and went to school in China from August 1995 until May 1996. He lived in Beijing with Zu Zeqing, who worked for his father's company. Beijing is the capital of China and one of the country's oldest and most historic cities.

Matt attended the sixth grade at a local school where he was one of only two students who were not Chinese. The other student was an Italian girl who had grown up in China. At school he was called Mai Xiu, Chinese for Matthew.

On the first day of class, Matt was the center of attention because he was so different from his Chinese classmates.

At first it was difficult for Matt that he looked and spoke differently from his Chinese classmates, but he soon made friends and adapted to life in China.

Some students even came up to him on the playground and touched his hair in amazement. This was because it was brown instead of dark black, like their own. When school ended that first day, about fifty students gathered around his desk. They stared at Matt and whispered among themselves about the new boy in their school. "My first encounter with being the different kid," [2] is how Matt describes the incident.

It is never easy to be the new student in school. It was especially difficult for Matt because he was so far away from his family and friends. But a situation that could have been lonely and frightening soon changed for the better because Matt was able to make new friends and adapt to life in China.

A Year Far from Home

During his year in China, Matt missed his family. He saw his father twice, but his mother visited only once, for two weeks. He never saw his brothers. "I remember being very lonely that first month," [3] Matt admits. To ease his loneliness, the young boy spent many hours looking at photographs of his family. He also had his parents send him his favorite music CDs. He enjoyed listening to them partly because they reminded him of home.

Zu Zeqing, whom Matt lovingly called "Aunt Zu," made him feel welcome in her home. She also introduced him to many people so he would not be so lonely. Some of them became Matt's best friends, and Matt also made new friends at school. One of his new friends was Liu Yingjie, the son of Liu Zhang, who was his teacher. "Aunt Zu and the friends I made were so wonderful that I eventually adjusted to being so far from home," [4] says Matt.

Matt enjoyed eating Chinese food, but was happy to discover a McDonald's restaurant in Beijing where he could have some food that reminded him of home.

It was also hard to go to a school in which everyone spoke **Mandarin,** a Chinese language that is very difficult to learn. Matt had learned some Mandarin before he went to China. But it was difficult to take classes in history, science, and mathematics that were taught in that language. One class, however, was easy for Matt—English. He said it was his favorite class because it was taught in English and he did not have to struggle to understand what the teacher was saying.

To relax and have fun, Matt played basketball and read books that his mother sent him. Matt loved reading so much that he had to be careful not to read too quickly. Otherwise, he might have run out of reading material before his mother could send him more books. "I read a ton," says Matt. "I guess that the books were my way of feeling like I was back home."[5]

Matt loved Chinese food, but even he got tired of eating Chinese meals every day. There were a few restaurants in Beijing that served Western food, including a McDonald's, but Matt had trouble getting some of his favorite foods. The two he dreamed about the most were pasta and ice cream.

Learning to Appreciate China

Matt enjoyed living in China because he learned so many new things about its language, traditions, and history—the things that make up a country's **culture**. Chinese culture is very different from that of the United States. Matt discovered that he liked many things about Chinese culture and that he could learn new ideas from it.

One of the most important lessons Matt learned during his year in China was that it is important to learn about the cultures of other countries. Says Matt: "I think that when people are exposed to different cultures, their view of the whole world becomes far richer. It has shaped my understanding of the world."[6]

Chapter Two

The Visit That Changed Matt Dalio's Life

M att Dalio returned home from the People's Republic of China in May 1996. Matt was happy to be back with his family and friends, and that fall he began attending Greenwich Country Day School. After completing the ninth grade at Greenwich he went to Brunswick School, a private high school.

Matt remained intensely interested in China even though he was thousands of miles away. He kept in contact with friends he had made there and enjoyed talking to people who had visited China or had some connection with that country. One of those conversations changed Matt's life.

Matt Decides to Help Chinese Orphans

In the spring of 2000 Matt talked to Lorraine Kennedy, a family friend who had adopted a baby girl from China. Kennedy told Matt how expensive and difficult it had been to adopt her daughter. She also described the orphanage in which the girl had lived. The orphanage had been very crowded because there were so many other children without parents. Kennedy also said there was not enough nutritious food for the children, too few workers to care for them, and shortages of medical supplies and items that infants needed, such as diapers.

Ever since he had returned from China, Matt had been searching for a way to repay the Chinese people for all the kind things they had done for him when he lived there. Kennedy's story made Matt realize what he could do for China. He says: "The Chinese people had been so wonderful to me, I wanted to do something to help them. After I

After hearing from a family friend about the difficulties she experienced while adopting a child from China, Matt knew he wanted to help the Chinese orphans and help smooth the adoption process.

talked to Kennedy, I knew that what I wanted to do was help orphans."[7]

The Chinese Orphan Problem

Matt returned to Beijing during his summer vacation in 2000 to learn about the problem of Chinese orphans so that he could figure out a way to help them. The first thing Matt discovered was that there were very many Chinese orphans. That was because of China's **one-child policy,** which allows each family to have only one baby.

China started the one-child policy in the 1970s to control its **population,** which is larger than any other country. China wanted to prevent its country from becoming so crowded that it would run out of living space and food for its people. In 2006 slightly more than 1.3 billion peo-

This billboard in China promotes the national one-child policy, which allows each family to have only one baby.

ple lived in China. That is more than four times the 300 million people who lived in the United States in that same year.

The one-child policy was meant to improve life for Chinese people. However, it accidentally created a huge number of orphans. China has never released an official figure on how many orphans the country has, but it is believed there are several million Chinese orphans. Almost all of the orphans are girls or children with physical or mental disabilities.

The one-child policy leads some couples to **abandon** female

The one-child policy in China has led to an increase in children being abandoned by their parents at the orphanages.

infants because they want a son. Male children have traditionally been favored in Chinese culture because of the emphasis on continuing the family line through future generations. When Chinese women married, they were considered part of their husband's family. Sons, however, remained part of the original family. They could continue the family name in the future by handing it down to their children. Another reason sons were valued is that they were expected to care for their parents as they grew older. However, most Chinese infants who become orphans today are those who are born with a disability. Couples abandon disabled infants because they want a healthy child. They also abandon such infants because many people cannot afford

Many Chinese orphanages are so overcrowded that they do not provide adequate play and living spaces for the children.

the medical care such children need to survive or to lead a normal life.

Conditions in Orphanages

Matt spent the month of July in China. He was helped by Zu Zeqing, with whom he had lived in 1995. Zu made arrangements for Matt to visit orphanages in Beijing and nearby cities and to meet with people who could explain the orphan situation.

One orphanage Matt visited was the Tianjin Children's Welfare Institute, which was home to 300 children. Matt was upset that the orphanage in Tianjin, a city near Beijing, was so small that the children there lived in extremely crowded conditions. He saw that as many as 30 boys and girls were jammed into a small space the size of a classroom in a U.S. school. They spent almost their entire day in that small room because there was no other place for them in the crowded orphanage. Says Matt: "Imagine living in a kindergarten classroom your whole life. That's what it was like."[8]

What touched Matt's heart most of all were the many disabled infants and children. The orphanages were not able to provide the medical care that could have cured minor physical defects or lessened more severe disabilities. For example, some children had cleft lips, which disfigured their faces and made it hard for them to talk properly. This medical condition can be easily fixed with surgery in the United States, but Chinese orphanages are unable to provide such care.

Matt knew that the disabilities doomed those children to growing up in orphanages because Chinese people would not adopt them or become their foster parents. This saddened Matt, who knew that growing up in an orphanage is not good for children. "No matter how good the conditions are, the children [in orphanages] are going to be starved for love,"[9] he says.

"How Could I Not Do That?"

The conditions Matt saw made him realize how lucky he was to have been born to parents who could care for

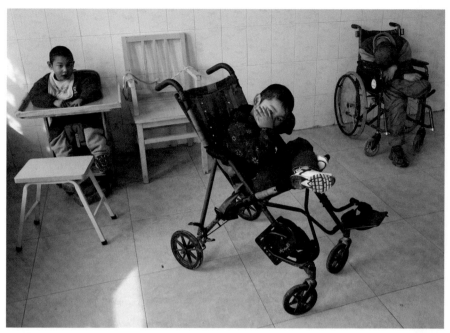

In China many orphanages are not able to provide the medical care that can cure minor physical defects or lessen more severe disabilities.

him and were able to give him a comfortable lifestyle. The teenager was so grateful for the blessings in his life that he felt compelled to help the less fortunate orphans. Says Matt: "Here I am in America with all of my needs met and they have nothing. If I could do something to help them, something to give those children hope, how could I not do that?"[10]

Chapter Three

Matt Dalio Turns His Dream into Reality

Matt Dalio returned from the People's Republic of China in the summer of 2000 with a dream of helping Chinese orphans. What Matt had learned about the orphan problem during his trip had convinced him that there were many things he could do to give Chinese orphans a better life. Matt knew that the key to helping the orphans was to raise money—a lot of money. He also knew that accomplishing that would not be an easy task for a sixteen-year-old.

Matt's Parents Help Him

Matt knew that to get enough money to help the orphans he needed to do something bigger than typical teenage fund-raising projects such as holding a bake sale or staging a car wash. He went to his parents for advice on how to raise funds for his **humanitarian** project.

When Matt told his mother and father he wanted to help Chinese orphans, his parents listened to him very seriously. Raymond and Barbara Dalio knew that their son was sincere in his desire to help those children. And because they believed Matt was capable of accomplishing such a difficult task, they assisted him in several ways.

The Dalios had many friends who were wealthy enough to make substantial contributions to Matt's project. They helped their son contact those friends, who became the first people to donate money to Matt's cause. Raymond Dalio also used his knowledge of financial matters and laws about how charitable foundations operate to help his son create China Care. With his help, Matt established the foundation in November 2000. "My parents were a huge help," Matt says.[11]

Matt Raises Money for China Care

Even though his parents helped Matt get started, he had to do the hardest part himself—he had to convince adults to give him money. Matt knew this would be difficult because the people he approached would wonder whether a teenager was smart enough to use their money wisely to help orphans in a far-off country. Says Matt: "I was 16 years old, so people thought, 'How is this kid going to do this?'"[12]

Some adults had such fears when Matt first contacted them. However, they soon realized how serious he was. Matt was also very persuasive in explaining the plight of Chinese orphans and how he would use the donated money to help those children. One method Matt used in asking for money was to have people calculate how much

Though only a teenager at the time, it was Matt's passion to help the orphans of China that convinced many people to initially donate to China Care.

their donation would be if it was divided by the number of days in a year. He would then tell potential donors, "For the cost of a latte a day, you can change a life." [13] This tactic made the donation seem small, and it helped Matt get bigger donations.

Lisa Valley, a neighbor in Greenwich, was one of his first contributors. She said Matt was so forceful and enthusiastic in asking for a donation that it was almost impossible to refuse him.

In just six months in 2000, Matt collected $70,000. Now that Matt had raised a significant amount of money, he had to decide how to use it to help Chinese orphans.

China Care Begins Helping Orphans

When Matt visited the Tianjin Children's Welfare Institute in July 2000, he learned that it was operating a program that enabled 200 children to live with foster families. Despite its one-child policy, the Chinese government allows families to care for up to three foster children.

To help more orphans experience the love of a family, China Care uses some of the money it raises to encourage Chinese families to foster children.

The government encourages families to do this by giving them money to help pay the cost of caring for the children. But because funds for the program were limited, many children who needed foster families had to remain in orphanages.

Matt decided to use the money he had raised to encourage more people to foster orphans. He did this because he believed orphans would be happier in foster homes. "That meant they would have real families and that's very important for children," [14] he says. And because children in China usually live with foster families until they are adults, children would be in the same home, with the same family, until they were old enough to care for themselves.

Matt needed someone who was living in China to help him set up the program. He once again turned to Zu Zeqing. Zu set up an office for China Care in Beijing. She then contacted orphanages and government officials so that the money Matt had collected could be used to place orphans in foster families. China Care was soon able to help fifty orphans move in with foster families.

A Busy Young Man

When Matt created China Care in 2000, he was a high school student at Brunswick School. Going to school and running China Care kept Matt so busy that he had to give up many activities most teenagers enjoy. Matt did find time for rock climbing and skiing. However, he had to quit the school's sailing team because he missed so many practices and competitions. He also had little spare time to surf the Internet, watch television, or learn new things like playing the guitar. Matt did not have much time for dating, but he did manage to go to his high school prom.

Matt admits that for a while "I sort of pitied myself for not being able to do things like that." [15] But he realized later that even though it kept him very busy, his experience with China Care was far more valuable than many of the fun things he had to skip. "In retrospect, I think that it was a blessing," he says. "I spent those years of my life learning about things that have far more meaning." [16] What Matt learned was that helping other people was more valuable and brought him more happiness than watching a TV show or having a good time in some other way.

Chapter Four

Making China Care Grow

In just a few months in 2000, Matt Dalio was able to raise $70,000 to help Chinese orphans. With that money, he was able to place fifty children in foster families and to provide some needed supplies and help to other Chinese orphans.

Dalio could have quit then, confident that he had repaid the Chinese people for the kind way they had treated him during the year he lived in China. His success, however, made him want to do even more. Dalio continued to devote himself to China Care, and in the next six years he helped it grow big enough to help thousands of orphans instead of just a few. The orphans received life-saving medical care, enjoyed better conditions at state-run orphanages, and were placed in new homes in China and the United States.

In an interview in 2006, Dalio said that even he was amazed at how much China Care had accomplished in six short years: "If I had set my sights for what we have today, people would have thought I was crazy. It has come a long way, far more than I could have imagined in my wildest dreams." [17]

Matt's Dream Grows Larger

When China Care began operating in November 2000, it was powered mostly by one teenager with a huge dream. By 2006 China Care had more than 200 employees in the United States and China. It had also developed a network of hundreds of students in high schools and colleges across the nation who raise funds for China Care and volunteer to help orphans in both countries.

Dalio graduated from Harvard University in June 2006 with a degree in psychology. He continued to head China Care even after he began working as a real estate investment analyst. As president of the charitable foundation, Dalio still visits China several times a year to oversee its operations there.

He is guided in running China Care by staff members and a **board of directors**. The directors include Zu Zeqing; his father, Raymond; and Lorraine Kennedy, the family friend who helped ignite his passion for Chinese orphans.

How China Care Helps Orphans

China Care focuses its work on orphans with physical and mental disabilities because they need help the most. It also works closely with the Chinese government to help all orphans by making repairs to run-down orphanages, funding foster families, and donating infant formula, diapers, and other supplies orphans need.

The organization Dalio founded has saved the lives of hundreds of desperately sick children by providing

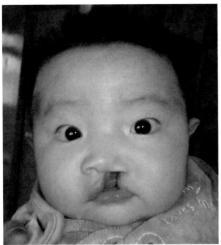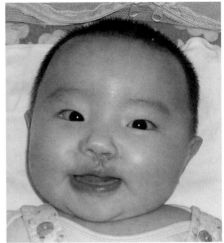

Dang Gui Ming, an orphan being cared for by China Care, is pictured before and after surgery to correct a cleft lip.

advanced medical care that Chinese orphanages cannot offer. They are treated at five China Care Children's Homes the group established in China. Medical personnel give children treatment and physical therapy for their disabilities. Doctors also use surgery to fix disabilities like a **cleft lip** or **clubfoot**.

The group also operates a foster family program. It matches disabled children with families and trains foster parents to care for the special needs of their new sons and daughters. It also helps people from the United States adopt disabled children. It gives the families financial assistance to help pay the cost of adoption, which can be as high as $20,000.

China Care, however, does not have enough money to help every disabled orphan. Dalio admits that in his role as the head of China Care, the toughest decisions he has to help make involve choosing the children who can have surgery or can be adopted. "It's like playing God sometimes," [18] Dalio says.

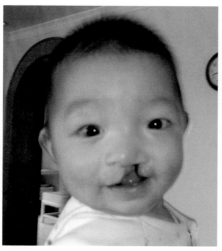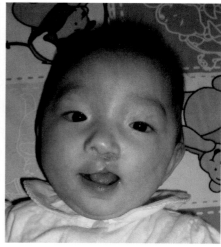

A cleft lip makes it hard to talk or chew properly. This is Dang Gui Yan before and after corrective surgery, provided for by China Care.

Raising Money to Help Orphans

As China Care grew, so did its need for money. Dalio could no longer raise enough funds by himself to pay for the work China Care was doing. To increase its funding, China Care began holding an annual charity dinner that featured famous entertainers like Sheryl Crow, B.B. King, and Carlos Santana. The dinners were a huge success. The 2006 event starred the Allman Brothers, Bonnie Raitt, and Branford Marsalis. It raised $1.2 million.

Many people have also donated money after learning about China Care through newspaper stories, magazine articles, and television shows. Most media coverage on China Care has focused on Dalio because so many people are amazed that a teenager started and runs a group that has helped so many Chinese orphans. Oprah Winfrey praised Dalio when he appeared on her show in 2002 and that same year *Teen People* magazine named him one of its "20 Teens Who Will Change the World."

Dalio was happy that this media attention increased donations but was uncomfortable that it was making him a celebrity. He told one newspaper reporter that he should write about why it is important to help orphans and not about Dalio himself. "China Care has become far more than just about myself," he said. [19]

But the media continues to be interested in Dalio because they know that without him, China Care would not exist today. They are also impressed that Dalio worked so hard to create the organization that he missed out on many fun things that other teenagers his age enjoy. What

Singer Bonnie Raitt, left, performed at China Care's 2006 charity dinner.

they may not know is that Dalio has no regrets about making those sacrifices to help Chinese orphans.

The Rewards Dalio Has Received

Dalio believes he has gained more than he has given up. His greatest reward has been to see the happiness he has brought to so many orphans. One of the orphans Dalio

The best part of Matt's work with China Care is the happiness he experiences when parents and children are brought together.

has helped is Grace, a Chinese girl who had a skin disease that produced black patches all over her body. Skin-graft surgery provided by China Care healed the blemishes, and in 2002 Kelly and Peter Liacopoulos of Grafton, Wisconsin, adopted her.

Dalio was at the airport when she arrived in the United States by plane to join her new family. He treasures the joy he saw that day. Says Dalio: "I remember the moment she arrived at the airport in America and hugged her dad for the first time. All she had ever looked for was family and there she had it." [20]

Dalio later became her godfather. He still visits her and says, "Close contact with Grace makes me see the magic of what we're doing." [21] In 2004 the Wisconsin couple adopted a second Chinese baby, this time a boy. In gratitude to Dalio, they named him Matt.

Chapter Five

What Young People Can Do to Help

When Matt Dalio first decided to help Chinese orphans, some adults probably believed he was too young and inexperienced to accomplish anything. Dalio proved them wrong by creating China Care, an organization that has made a difference in the lives of thousands of Chinese orphans.

Dalio believes that many young people today have the same doubts about themselves as adults did about him. "They don't realize the impact they can have,"[22] Dalio says of teenagers. But Dalio is committed to helping young people realize that they can do important things before they become adults.

"Do It! Just Start!"

One of the most important ways in which Dalio encourages young people is by being a role model. His accomplishments when he was a teenager make other teens realize that they can also do something important. And Dalio spends a lot of time trying to convince young people that they have the power to make a difference in their world. "China Care's second mission," Dalio says, "is to empower youth. I want to make kids know that they can do big things at any age." [23] Dalio repeats that message over and over in talks to young people and in interviews with the news media.

Despite his own success, Dalio understands that it is not easy for young people to be brave enough to tackle a big project like he did. He knows young people may worry that others, both adults and kids their own age, will doubt

Matt Dalio is pictured with a group of China Care children and their nannies on his spring 2005 trip to China.

that they can do something significant to change the world like he did. Dalio also believes that many young people hesitate to tackle such projects because they doubt they can accomplish their goals. His advice to young people with ambitious goals is simple—forget those fears and just go ahead with the project they have picked. Says Dalio: "Do it! Just start! It is always daunting when you look at what other people have done, but as soon as you start, you realize that it is not that hard. The toughest part is just getting the ball rolling. From there, the snowball keeps building." [24]

Dalio realizes more than almost anyone else how much young people can accomplish when they work hard. He has even harnessed some of that power to help China Care.

China Care Youth Groups

Dalio took his mission of helping Chinese orphans with him when he began attending Harvard University. His work so impressed some of his classmates that they founded China Care Harvard. Members of the college club raised funds for China Care and a few went to China as volunteers to work in orphanages. The club also began a program to bring together adopted children and their parents who live in the same area. The children can play with other Chinese kids and parents can discuss some of the problems of raising Chinese orphans, such as how to help their children learn about their Chinese culture.

The club concept quickly spread to other colleges. In 2006 there were more than twenty clubs scattered across

Inspired by Matt's work, teenager Jack Rivers (left), became a China Care volunteer and has raised thousands of dollars for the cause.

the nation at schools like Yale, Brown, Keuka, and Northwestern.

High school students have also helped Chinese orphans. One was Jack Rivers, who, like Dalio, lived in Greenwich, Connecticut. Inspired by Dalio, the fifteen-year-old Rivers raised $28,000 for China Care in 2004. He made a personal appeal to members of Stanwich Congregational Church, which he attended, and sent out letters to other people requesting donations. That summer Rivers also spent five weeks painting and fixing up an orphanage in China.

In April 2006 students at the Latin School of Chicago raised $11,000 for China Care by hosting a fashion show. Young people, however, do not have to gather huge sums of money to help Chinese orphans. They can sponsor a single orphan for just $39 a month. The money helps pay for basic living costs such as food, medical care, and school tuition. And donations of any amount can be used to buy supplies that orphanages and China Care homes need to care for children.

Another China Care Goal

China Care has accomplished a great deal since Dalio started it in 2000. In its first six years, China Care helped more than 100 U.S. families adopt children, placed several hundred children in Chinese foster families, and saved the

In 2006 Chinese president Hu Jintao, right, met with U.S. president George W. Bush during the Asia-Pacific Economic Cooperation forum in Hanoi, Vietnam.

lives of hundreds of boys and girls who had severe medical problems.

But even though China Care's main purpose will always be to help orphans, Dalio thinks it can accomplish another important goal. Like the Chinese orphans who are adopted by families in the United States, Dalio himself feels like someone who belongs to both countries. Because Dalio loves both China and his homeland, he would like to see the two countries become friendlier.

Dalio knows that will not be easy because China and the United States were once political enemies. In the 1950s the two nations even fought each other during the Korean War. But Dalio believes that the work China Care does will help individuals in China and the United States understand each other better and realize that there are good people in both countries. "One of my goals," Dalio says, "is to let people on both sides know how amazing the people on the other side are." [25] When that happens, Dalio believes the governments of the two nations will have an easier time cooperating and doing things together to benefit both countries and the rest of the world.

Notes

Introduction: Helping Those Who Need Help the Most
1. Matt Dalio, interview with the author, October 1, 2006.

Chapter One: Matt Dalio Learns to Love China
2. Dalio, interview.
3. Dalio, interview.
4. Dalio, interview.
5. Dalio, interview.
6. Dalio, interview.

Chapter Two: The Visit That Changed Matt Dalio's Life
7. Dalio, interview.
8. Quoted in Dana Schmidt, "Adoption Angels," *Family Circle,* November 9, 2004, p. 19.
9. Quoted in Schmidt, "Adoption Angels," p. 19.
10. Quoted in ABC News, "Person of the Week: Matt Dalio, Harvard Student Gives Chinese Orphans New Hope," December 24, 2004. www.abcnews.go.com/WNT/PersonOfWeek/story?id=355944&page=1.

Chapter Three: Matt Dalio Turns His Dream into Reality
11. Dalio, interview.
12. Quoted in Neil Vigdor, "Stars Shine at Belle Haven Fund-raiser," *Greenwich Time,* September 11, 2004, p. A1.

13. Quoted in Joseph P. Kahn, "A Bridge to China: Harvard Junior Matt Dalio's Foundation Goes the Distance for Orphans," *Boston Globe,* September 11, 2004, p. C1.

14. Dalio, interview.

15. Dalio, interview.

16. Dalio, interview.

Chapter Four: Making China Care Grow

17. Dalio, interview.

18. Quoted in Neil Vigdor, "Santana Performs to Help China Care," *Greenwich Time,* June 20, 2005, p. A3.

19. Quoted in Vigdor, "Stars Shine at Belle Haven Fundraiser," p. A1.

20. Quoted in ABC News, "Person of the Week: Matt Dalio."

21. Quoted in Joseph P. Kahn, "A Bridge to China."

Chapter Five: What Young People Can Do to Help

22. Quoted in Nicole Rivard, "Making the World a Better Place," *Greenwich Citizen,* September 10, 2004, Living Section.

23. Dalio, interview.

24. Dalio, interview.

25. Quoted in Ivana V. Katic, "Harvard China Care Provides Comfort to Adopted Children," *Harvard Crimson,* March 1, 2004. www.thecrimson.com/ article.aspx?ref=357868.

Glossary

abandon: To leave behind; in China, couples who cannot care for infants leave them in public places so they will be taken to orphanages.

adopt: To legally become the parent(s) of a child born to someone else.

board of directors: A group of people who advise a business or charitable group on its operations.

charitable foundation: An organization dedicated to helping people.

cleft lip: A deformed lip that makes it hard to talk.

clubfoot: A deformed foot that makes it hard to walk.

culture: The set of beliefs and traditions shared by people who live in a country.

disabilities: Physical or mental conditions that make it hard or even impossible for a person to do things other people can, such as walk, hear, or see.

foster families: Families that care for children who were born to someone else, without legally adopting the children.

humanitarian: To do something for people who need help; to aid humanity.

investments: Money given to a business to earn more money.

Mandarin: The official language of China.

one-child policy: The Chinese law that restricts families to having just one child.

orphanages: Government-run homes in which orphans live.

orphans: Children who have no living parents or who have been abandoned by their parents.

population: The total number of people who live in a country, state, or city.

For Further Exploration

Books

Debbie Blackington and Brynne Blackington, *Mama's Wish/Daughter's Wish*. Duxbury, MA: Pebbleton, 2004. A mother and the Chinese girl she adopted both tell their story in this picture book.

Karin Evans, *The Lost Daughters of China*. New York: Tarcher, 2000. The author explains how she adopted a Chinese baby and discusses cultural reasons that lead Chinese families to abandon female and disabled babies.

Robert Green, *China*. San Diego, CA: Lucent, 1999. This author explains the history, geography, and culture of the People's Republic of China.

Jean MacLeod, *At Home in This World: A China Adoption Story*. Warren, NJ: EMK, 2003. In this story, written by the parent of two Chinese children, a nine-year-old girl explains what it is like to be an adopted child in the United States.

Web Sites

China Adoption, Adoption.com (http://china. adoption.com). This site has a wide range of information on various aspects of adopting Chinese babies as well as links to other sites.

China Care (www.chinacare.org). The official site for China Care has information on its programs and how people can help it care for Chinese orphans.

China Internet Information Center (www.china.org.cn). This Internet site operated by the Chinese government has news about China and basic information about Chinese history, politics, economics, and culture including how to speak Chinese.

Families with Children from China (www.fwcc.org). This site provides resources for families that have adopted Chinese orphans.

Video

China's Lost Girls, DVD. National Geographic Video, 2005. This video examines issues about adoption and China's one-child policy designed to curb the country's exploding population.

Index

Picture Credits

About the Author

Michael V. Uschan has written more than fifty books, including *Life of an American Soldier in Iraq*, for which he won the 2005 Council for Wisconsin Writers Juvenile Nonfiction Award. It was the second time he won the award. Uschan began his career as a writer and editor with United Press International, a wire service that provides stories to newspapers, radio, and television. Journalism is sometimes called "history in a hurry," and Uschan considers writing history books a natural extension of the skills he developed in his many years as a journalist. He and his wife, Barbara, reside in the Milwaukee suburb of Franklin, Wisconsin.